CONTRACTORS: **Doing it Right** Not Just Getting it Done

Construction Companies Using Their Culture to Influence the Perception of Their Brand

Mel DePaoli

BRAND or CULTURE
PUBLISHING

To seeing connections where the connections appear all but invisible, the world is not always as it seems.

Many thanks to all who supported, encouraged, participated, and challenged me.

First Printing February 2010, Second Printing December 2010

ISBN-10: 0-9844344-0-2

ISBN-13: 978-0-9844344-0-4

Contents

www.ContractorsDoingItRight.com

Foreword: Woman-Owned, Coachable & Successful

Knowing the importance of the hard-to-define culture of our company has helped us not only survive, but thrive these last twenty five years. I've often wondered why so few books have been written about culture, as in my opinion, it is the key to business success.

Business culture is especially critical in the world of residential remodeling. Our typical client is often home, watching every move of our employees. Working in a "fish bowl" environment requires the highest level of professional performance on a consistent basis. This may help explain the less-than-stellar regard that is given to our industry at large, as very few people in the construction world can take that kind of pressure.

Starting out with absolutely no business training, I had to learn the technical aspects as well as the business aspects of becoming a remodeler. Having been a former high school teacher and leader of a 5 piece traveling band, I had an established knowledge and framework of how to set goals, motivate drummers and students and influence the behavior of others. Performing music gigs for 5 years straight night after night, town after town, also helped me learn how to perform and deliver, come what may. (If I never enter a bar again, much less play for happy hour,

I will not feel deprived. I have done my "time".) Through these life experiences, I learned invaluable lessons about group communication and cooperation, ethical leadership, living a principled life and earning an "honest living." These are values that we constantly and consistently emphasize at Harrell Remodeling.

Along the way, I've had amazing people to help me grow our business. My lifetime partner and now wife, Ann Benson, supported me while I learned the trades and how to run a business. Her mother was my first paying client and represented the ideal customer prototype I was looking for--someone who was very particular, had high expectations, and appreciated the small things that make a business great, like frequent, clear communication, a really clean jobsite and a schedule that was adhered to. My mother-in-law's best friend knew a retired carpenter named Chape, who became a father figure for me and taught me more than I could ever convey. With Chape, I not only learned how to wield a hammer and skill saw, but I realized I had the courage and conviction to start a woman-owned remodeling company and that my previous experiences supported my abilities to do so.

Over the years, my mentors appeared like angels each time I was ready to grow my company to the next level. Early on, I joined a newly-formed business peer group and Harrell Remodeling has continued to be involved in this indispensable support system for 20 of the 25 years we have been in business in California. I could not have been successful without those peer groups or without the people who believed in me and coached me each step of the way. One saving grace I had was that I learned to be "coachable." This helped me progress more quickly than some of my peers, who felt too vulnerable when challenged with new paradigm shift or when progress required a major change in their way of leadership.

If I had been given this book to read and study when I started my remodeling business, I would be even further along in my business development. Allow this book to be your coach while building your business and learn to *do it right—not just get it done!*

Iris Harrell

Harrell Remodelling

Foreword: Are You Different?

When author Mel DePaoli decided to write this book her timing could not have been better. Her company Omicle continues to focus on Brand or Culture in American business and whether Brand or Culture is the driving force behind why some companies continue to be successful over time and others just exist or eventually fail?

Midway through writing this book, all of America became challenged with the worst economic cycle since October 1929. Contractors were among those industries first and hardest hit. By the time this book publishes we will all have personally dealt with these most difficult times. There were extremely hard decisions that tested ourselves, our relationships, and whether we could actually survive the unknown that lay ahead. Owners and managers could no longer instinctively and strategically look 1 3 years ahead, and had to deal with day to day realities. I think we could all agree that what we have learned from our recent experiences emerging from this cycle and what we do as a result will lay the foundation for our futures, those of our customers, our team members, their families and all future generations in America who should rely on us to do what is right long-term and not what is best right now for our pocketbook. The fact that you have this book is testament to your intentions.

America is still the greatest country in the world. Yes

America is being tested right now. Certainly our elected officials, Wall Street corporations, banking, investment and other systems are under huge public and international scrutiny at present for their past decisions. I would submit however, that a large part of what has always made America great is that entrepreneurial individuals have always started and ran businesses, held fast to their dreams, worked hard, remained honest, accepted the risks, met their payrolls, provided quality products and services, and paid close attention to who they were, who their customers were and how they should be treated.

All too often "Big Corporation" makes decisions at the highest uninvolved corporate level, based on numbers, what the definition of their relationship with their customers and employees are and then expect their employees to accept this definition and deal with it whether they like it or not.

Unlike "Big Corporation," team members in our companies are not viewed as expendable commodities; they are an asset that we can continue to invest in and the reason our companies can and continue to achieve consistent, measurable success over time. The timing of Mel's newest book gave us an opportunity to re-verify where we came from, where we are at, who we are, what we believe, what we do, and what we can do better. If our companies do not have future value then they will not continue to be here.

All products and services can be designed, engineered, built, marketed and delivered to either rise up to a certain quality or expectation level or to drop down to a certain price point. The old adage, "You get what you pay for" seems appropriate here.

Whether you are an independent business owner or a corporate owned business manager this fundamental decision must be made. Yes the experience and product received can be augmented by exciting marketing, attractive finance terms or smart packaging, but in the end the product gets used by the customer and they make a real life decision whether to purchase it again or recommend others to purchase it, based on their experiences, value received and what the company that sold it to them really represents to them.

Residential development and homebuilding are still among the highest failure rate businesses in America and after almost 27 years of continued daily hands on involvement in this industry, I will submit that our companies Mission Statement and Customer Philosophy are not simply words on a website. They truly are what we believe in and what we guide ourselves by each and every day with each customer.

Perhaps customer expectations have been dumbed down in America in substitution for ever lower prices and faster delivery cycles. If so then should we not endeavor to deliver higher customer focus to exceed these current day lowered expectations? Will this effort ultimately equate to higher customer satisfaction ratings, more new customers who enthusiastically produce more referrals and increase the value of your relationships with them and your companies resultant increased brand value? Our experience says yes but we will let Mel tell you more about that.

I sincerely thank Mel DePaoli for writing this book and for reminding American business owners and managers to allow their companies to look in the mirror and assess themselves honestly. I personally hope that within these pages you will be inspired to implement positive changes to your business internally that reflect the changes your company is experiencing externally. Any economic cycle is a great time to re-invest in your company's future. What happens next is up to each of us individually and for that I am glad you are truly different and wish to *thrive and not just survive.*

Steve Klein

The Klein Companies

Foreword: Handcuffed to the Front Door

In the early to mid-1990's I began to make a deliberate effort to lead our company culture in a direction that would allow me to not be "handcuffed to the front door" of our business inhibiting me from pursuing other interests. I had spent several years "handcuffed to the front door" of my business in which most of the day to day business activities had to go through me. As a result, I was literally being mentally and physically handcuffed to the business.

Luckily, there weren't too many years like that which ultimately leads to a cynical, burnt out, business owner—an all too familiar story; living inside a scenario in which your business becomes your only identity and consumes almost your entire existing, leaving no mental or physiological capacity for any other interests including family and personal, eventually sucks the life blood out of having any passion for your business or your life.

Don't get me wrong. I'm not talking about not working long and hard at your business, especially when your business needs you. Nor am I talking about becoming a totally disconnected, absentee owner who no longer knows what is going on with his business. Nor having some delusional dream that one day your business is going to operate all by itself and that you can become totally irrelevant while they keep sending you bigger and bigger checks every week. That is the equivalent of an investor in a business which could eventually be your business, but that is another story entirely. What I am referring to now is how you being the leader of your business and the culture of your company can help shape your life inside that business and outside that business.

The first turning point for me was my desire to reside in San Diego for three months every winter. My wife, Mary, has a very large family, most of who live in San Diego, and we wanted to spend time there so that we, and especially our children, Heather and Thomas, could grow up having a relationship with their west coast grandparents, aunts, uncles, and cousins. We did this for six years, from 1996 through 2001. While away I was still in touch by phone, fax, and email, just in a different state; at the time that was a huge leap for me since I had always been there with the exception of an occasional vacation.

In order to achieve this living arrangement, I had to develop systems and a culture that would allow for me to be away from my business for three months at a time. My focus was to attract and train people who could, in essence, run their position in the company more independently than the average person who requires more supervision. For years I shared the book *Going from Good to Great* by Jim Collins in our annual company kick-off meetings, which speaks about getting the right people on the bus and in the right seat on the bus, and getting the wrong people off the bus. The right people for our company are people who can think and act independently enough to make decisions without having to be micromanaged in order to accomplish the majority of their work and, more specifically, don't need to approach me with low and mid-level decisions. The individual first works out their issue either on their own or by sharing it with other team members or a manager prior to it ever having to come my way. As a result, most things never even get to me unless it involves a higher level decision. This frees up a tremendous amount of time for me to work on things that are the highest and best use of my time and interests. This cultural pursuit has been well over a fifteen year journey that has served my company, Capizzi Home Improvement, in business since 1976, very well.

The initial six years of wintering in San Diego led to my second turning point, putting the company and culture to the test when I moved to southwest Florida full-time for almost four years, from 2002 to 2005, in an effort to expand our real estate and development interests in Florida and Costa Rica.

My third turning point occurred between 2006 and 2007 when I pursued another interest and a long awaited passion of mine, to enter the sport of auto racing, which took me away for eight weeks a year, on top of all of my other endeavors. All of this would not have been possible without constantly pursing a company culture made up of many self-reliant team members with an entrepreneurial spirit.

The idea of "being handcuffed to the front door of your

business" is mostly psychological. You first have to remove the psychological handcuffs in order to actually let go a little; delegate to good people and empower them to do more. Your commitment to repeat this cycle, once it takes hold, will be liberating.

I first met Mel at a conference put on by Certified Contractors Network® where I sat in on a panel in which Mel moderated a Q & A session on company culture and brand. I believe the reason Mel and I connected so well is because we both have a passion and commitment to the all-important topic of company culture. I encourage you to read and reread this book because it brilliantly outlines the importance of creating the right company culture for you and your business. Start the liberating process here.

Tom Capizzi, Jr.
Capizzi Home Improvement

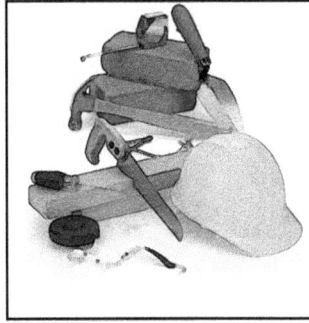

Preface

Companies that develop and work to maintain strong cultures consistently outperform companies that do not. While this idea may not seem to be connected with the more conventional wisdom of creative marketing, strong sales, good products and service, and branding that most of us consider being the elements of a successful business, I assure you they are quite connected. If you want a sustainable business that runs itself, is consistently innovative and flexible enough to adapt and change as the times do, you must consider culture.

Every industry has companies that set the standard for excellent work environments. In construction, there are a growing number of companies that are working hard to raise the bar for their industry. In my opinion, leaders of this movement include Steve Klein, Iris Harrell, and Tom Capizzi, Jr. In my two years of research, I have lost count how many times their names have come up as "someone I need to meet" or "I wish I could be them."

The construction industry is critical to economic growth; the foundation that creates the potential for all other industries. It's an industry that still relies on skills and traditions from the past while constantly investigating and embracing the change and advancement necessary to move into the future. Because of how important this industry is and the potential it holds, I started researching construction firms before the downturn in the economy. I wanted to get a better understanding of the industry's true potential and why it seemed that potential was not being well-leveraged.

More than 30 construction companies voluntarily participated in my research, which was a requirement for potential inclusion in this book. In order to take part, they had to meet three criteria:

- *Minimum of 15 employees (not including any subcontractors they use)*
- *Minimum of five years in business, and*
- *Minimum of $1 million in revenue.*

The research itself included:

- *Completing a detailed company profile.*
- *Minimum of three interviews, and*
- *A custom survey distributed to the employees.*

The companies provided me with snapshots of overall operations that included the past three years of financial information, monies spent on education and training of employees, and budgetary information dealing with marketing. I also wanted to see how they described their companies in terms of messaging and branding, and how they defined their target markets without being prompted.

Three interviews were required to obtain a holistic view of the company. I interviewed the owners or CEOs, the CMOs or Marketing Directors, and midlevel managers, usually a team lead or production manager. All interviewees were asked the same base questions and encouraged to answer with whatever came top of mind. Top of mind answers were key as those answers tended to be the most honest and reflected up to date information and impressions.

The customized employee surveys included specific terms used by management and the beliefs they expressed in the interviews. My goal was to learn whether what management said/believed reflected reality within the company. Most of the surveys were distributed online, but because of the nature of the job, some had to be distributed the old fashioned way—via paper. Participating companies needed to complete all requirements to be considered as 'valid.'

The results were enlightening. Some companies dropped out before completing the process, while others were so engaged they immediately made changes and implemented new strategies that were suggested. Management with those companies that discontinued participation often were hesitant about releasing the employee survey; perhaps fearing the results. Those that completed the process said they found it to be rewarding and many of them even used the outcomes as the foundation for internal company reviews.

Another interesting element that affected production of this book was the economy. About three quarters of the way through the interviews, the market crashed. The construction industry was among the first and hardest affected. Truly testing both the companies' culture and sustainability, the economic downturn revealed the real industry winners. And it is those stories and examples that are used in this book.

Each chapter or section focuses on one particular aspect of culture, brand, and the connection between them. I've included case studies to help convey particular points and practices that others can use to position themselves for the economic turnaround, and applaud them for surviving the worst economic downturn since the Great Depression.

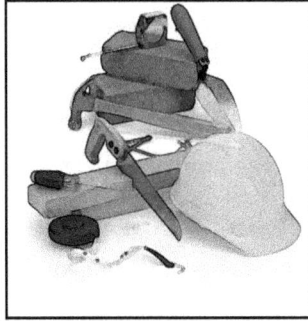

A Moment On Cultures

The culture of a company defines and explains the missing link. It is comprised of everything that happens in day to day, moment to moment affairs that the majority of people do not consider. It influences how employees approach or handle every situation. It's a pattern of the feelings, thoughts, and basic assumptions that drive everything within the company and how the company approaches the market.

That said, a company's culture is not all touchy-feely. A successful culture is made up of strategic elements, actions, and processes. It is a choice that needs to be made and reinforced every day. The touchy-feely aspect is simply a byproduct of a lot of hard work.

With something this powerful, it is amazing it does not command more of a focus. Identifying and understanding the potential is still a mainly underground talent. But the companies that do invest the time, money, and effort into their culture have rewards that other companies only dream about. They have learned that a company cannot survive and thrive by the numbers alone. The true value of having a strong culture is the ability to perform consistently over the long-term.

For the purpose of these interviews, I defined culture as, "the beliefs and values within a company or organization that influence the following: how decisions are made, processes, procedures, company policies, and interaction between employees." Since the companies that were being interviewed, were already aware of the purpose, I felt this definition was as it needed to be.

A company's roots are what define its mission, value, and vision statements. Understanding the original and current goals of the company lay the groundwork for the company's culture, purpose and sometimes even execution. A common mistake is allowing the core values and the core purpose of the company to become simply words on paper or on the wall and not acting to ensure those words actually reflect the culture of the company. The culture is how these words are brought to life—how these words affect the people within your organization, your clients, vendors and the market. Communication, rituals, and processes are how the mission, values, and visions come alive to create the culture of the company and also influence how it is maintained. These elements create focus and shape behavior which lays the groundwork for how your company will be perceived.

A company's culture is dynamic; most have sub-cultures within the main. The challenge is in choosing to create, and then maintaining a cohesive culture that ensures your employees can work together as a unified team.

Turning Points & Beyond

In almost every successful company I spoke with, the owner experienced an epiphany about their lives and/or business which started a turning point for the company. When they started their business, they operated one way, and then something happened which lead them to change almost everything about how the company operates, and opened their eyes to the value of building and maintaining a strong culture.

Invariably what triggered the owner's epiphany was a truly life changing event. This event was so powerful that they could recall every last detail and emotion that accompanied it; time stood still while they looked around and realized that everything was wrong and they were on the path to failure unless something changed.

Let's take a look at some of the moments that changed these companies forever. Here are their stories.

Turning Point #1: Trying to Let Go. "The first time

I promoted someone else as President was a huge disaster. What I ended up learning was that the people who were able to take the company to the growth point were not the same people who were going to take it to the next level. They didn't want to go to the next level. The difference was that I had grown and my employees I had at the time, had not. I had to clean house and start over. [When I hired my next team,] I purposely hired people with different backgrounds than my own and the company's. It is working this time."

"It was my own immaturity that held the company back. I had to learn that my employees are not my family, and that I must be professional first. You can be warm, respectful, friendly, and professional, but if you have to fire someone, you need to be able to fire them. I had to learn that you have to be professional first and hire a more mature group who is able to help the company grow."

Turning Point #2: Market Change. "When we changed the products we sold. We didn't intend on going after a more affluent market, but a top of the line product demanded it. This required that we change our image, our marketing and our target market. The company image and marketing we had at the time did not appeal to our new market. We also had to change how we interacted with our clients. This new market had different expectations of us so we had to make changes to become a team. Before the company was segregated with animosity, now we are one team."

Turning Point #3: Life Threatening Illness. "The

owner of our company got cancer and two of our relatively new employees stepped up to grow the company in a short period of time. This allowed the owner to focus on his treatments and getting better while being reassured that his business would still be here when he returned. This also showed him that he was able to delegate work and it would be accomplished. The business was able to grow in a slightly different way than was originally intended."

Turning Point #4: Finding Their Client. "During a presentation I attended on branding, the speaker asked: How do you know who your client is? How do you get to those people? What do you say when you get to them?"

"When he asked these three key questions, I realized that I could not answer them. I left the meeting with the emptiest feeling in my stomach. It was my job to know the answer and I didn't. Later, I realized that throughout his presentation he talked about a roadmap to answering those very questions. I was so excited, I asked the presenter to meet with us and walk us through the process. This turned on a flood light for us with a beacon pointing in the right direction. We realized that it would take time, money and effort to identify who we were and who our real clients are and it is worth every bit of it. In the end, we had something tangible that would be of value to our clients. We found out what our clients valued in us and we now use that to communicate to future clients."

Turning Point #5: Legal Trouble. "I had a client who wouldn't pay their bill so I had to go to a lawyer. Through this process, a disgruntled employee was discovered and made accusations about the company doing fraud. I was searched and seized because of this. This whole process took three years. After this, I put systems in place that allowed workers to pick who they worked with. I also made sure we were always upfront with clients about costs. It created a better work environment and built a stronger company. My time going through this, allowed me to define our target market and the type of people we want to work for and with. We did prevail and they sided with us."

After hearing all of these turning point stories, what was your turning point moment?

The key to remember here is that all companies go through ups and downs. It is to be expected and prepared for. Down times provide you an opportunity to tighten up loose ends and fix what needs fixing. It's the time you always ask for when everyone in your company is running around like a chicken with their head cut off because they are so busy. The down times and the turning points are the time to prepare your company for growth in the next new economy even when they come at inconvenient times.

Turning points are most often influenced or created by an external force that is also instrumental in moving the company to the next level. This is your business. You and your team know it better than anyone, but realistically there are times when you are too close to see what needs to be improved or how to improve it properly.

When the owners interviewed had their turning point, they explained their experience as very emotional. Each of them even admitted there was even a point when their mind went blank . . .

They thought, "What do we need to change? Who can tell me what to change? Who can help me make the changes? Do we need to change our marketing? Who should I hire? Why should we hire them? Do we need to change where we market? Do we need to change who we market to? Do we need more sales people? Do we need more carpenters? We need more clients. How do we know who our clients are? How do we get in front of them? What are we going to do? How are we going to solve this? How are we going to have a business in the future? How are we going to keep from going under?"

. . . these are just some of the questions that ran through their mind.

Once their mind calmed down enough to think clearly, this is where they realized they needed help because what they were doing was no longer going to work and no one who helped them in the past was going to be able to help them through this. The new sources of help varied for each company. For some it was joining a construction organization. Others hired a consultant. For others it was hiring an employee, or many new employees with different skills and attributes than what they had previously looked for.

All of these solutions are correct because they all stemmed from reaching beyond the leaders' comfort zone into an area that was new. While each path is different, there are three commonalities to making the transition a success.

1. Being open and honest with everyone on your team. Turning points are normally so big that you could not hide them if you tried, but nevertheless this is a great time to set the stage for a new reality. As the owner, you must trust your employees with sensitive information before they will trust you with the impending changes.

Being open and honest with your team means admitting you do not know everything and acknowledge that you are reaching out for help. The help you are receiving will affect your employees, how jobs are done and how the business is run. Being open and honest also provides you the opportunity to learn from your employees. Like kids, they see things and they know things you did not think they would. Learn from them so they will be open to learning from you. It is your job to demonstrate trust.

2. At least half of the team that got the company to the current point most likely will leave. This ends up being a pain point, one that many of the owners wished they knew going into the transition. They agreed that they still would have proceeded, but they would have been more prepared if they had known to expect it. Sometimes it is key employees that will leave. Employees stay when they feel like they fit but a lot of people have a hard time with change. As you go through all of the changes it will be just as hard if not harder on them, than it is for you. Losing these employees is often what the company needs to move forward so you can bring in the employees that will take you to the next level.

3. *The process will take a lot of time—think one to three years with a lot of changes simultaneously.* Yes there is a lot of valid advice out there about making incremental changes to improve a company so you are not overwhelmed by them. However, that advice is aimed at sustaining a successful stable company, not one going through the process to become one.

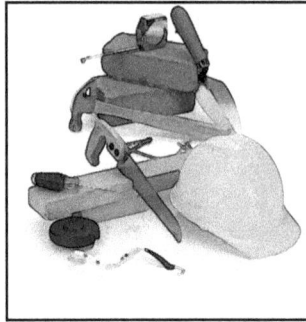

Snowflake Syndrome

The label says it all! Snowflakes are admired for their uniqueness, but that quality is lost when a snowflake is just one of hundreds or thousands. Yes, a single snowflake is unique and beautiful, but to someone in the middle of a snowstorm (or faced with a wide choice of suppliers) it looks like all the other ones falling around them. Companies that suffer from Snowflake Syndrome believe they are unique in their market and that the market should recognize them for it. They often forget that to the market they look no different than the hundreds of other companies in their space.

Businesses go through various phases as they develop and grow. Snowflake Syndrome often appears in businesses at specific stages of growth: startup, about two to four years after a turning point moment and at the launch of a new product or service from an established company. These are stages when a company is adjusting to a new way or direction and there is an odd mix of vulnerability and ego.

When a company first starts to settle on and accept a new way, approach or belief, but lacks experience to effectively deal with drastic changes and their effects, their culture is best described as immature. In this state, there are still frequent changes, and there is a strong need for company-wide education.

A company's culture begins to mature after about five years. At this stage, a company 'has a feel,' employees instinctually 'know the way things are done', and changes are subtle and happen over time.

One thing that quickly stood out as a stark difference between companies with mature cultures and those with less developed cultures was the perception of their business in the marketplace and the role their cultures served.

Companies with mature cultures described their culture as the driving force of their success—inwardly focused, they work consistently to maintain and improve their culture. When they looked outward they were less interested in comparing themselves to others and more focused on gleaning new concepts and techniques to advance their own cultures.

Companies with immature cultures often fell victim to Snowflake Syndrome. They invariably described their company as if it were the only one in the world to operate their business in an ethical, legal manner where the employees are valued and appreciated. They spoke as if their company was a unique and beautiful snowflake that the market should easily be able to pick out from a blizzard of businesses. Instead of looking inward, they either copied others, hoping to piggyback on their success, or belittled them hoping to make themselves look more favorable to the market.

Harsh words, but accurate. During the interviews, I specifically asked these companies if they knew of any other company that also focused on their culture. I even encouraged them to think outside of construction. Almost every time the answer was "No," they couldn't seem to think of a single company that understands the value of their culture. And yet, there are plenty of companies out there who are famous for it and who take pride in maintaining a strong culture. Companies like: IBM, Disney, Google, Microsoft, Southwest, Wegmans, and Pike Place Fish Market—hardly unknowns in the marketplace.

These companies vary in size, industry, target market, and approach. There is no single template to creating a strong company culture. There is no one way to build it or maintain it, but there are many ways to leverage its power.

The self-delusion companies with immature cultures suffered from ultimately lead to some rather nasty surprises as they moved through the evaluation process. They were shocked at what their survey results revealed—that in reality, they did not have as strong or consistent a culture as they thought! Some companies seized the opportunity, considered the results and implemented suggestions that were made, while others faded into the background and let the economy take the blame.

Don't get me wrong, I am well aware of the severity of the economic crash at the time of this writing and how it affected this industry in particular. I do understand that it took out many companies and hurt even more. But there were many stories most people never heard about: contractors that were incredibly busy, that were having the best year in the history of the company or some that did not downsize to hunker down or die, but rather to launch a new section of their business. Rather than use the economy as an excuse, they looked objectively at the elements they had control over and made sure they were as strong as they needed to be. An integral part of this was considering what others were doing, rather than seeing themselves as unique (making their problems unique and thus intractable!).

All of that said, your company is special—a unique snowflake. However, remember that just because a company has a different culture from yours does not mean that one of you is wrong, or that there is nothing you can learn from each other. Each of you has elements of your culture that work for your company. This is very important to understand so let me repeat: just because a company has a different culture than yours does not mean that one of you is wrong. You are just different, and there is always something to learn from others. Like snowflakes, businesses are unique, but unlike snowflakes they are not static crystals, they can change, and most importantly, they can borrow ideas from other companies and incorporate them in ways that are still unique to them.

On the flip side, a huge mistake that many of business owners make is copying instead of learning a concept and adapting it to their way of doing things and applying it to their need. Avoiding the negative effects of the Snowflake Syndrome is not about copying someone else's business. Learn from others—their strengths, their ways of doing things and resolving issues, and integrate what you learned into your own company. But remember to honor your company's own strengths. No company is 100% wrong or screwed up, just as no company is 100% right and perfect. There is an old saying: "your team is never as bad as they look when they screw up or as good as they look when they succeed." The same is true for companies.

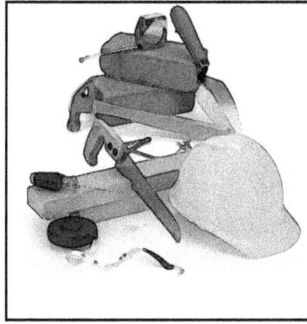

The Cost of Culture

The construction industry has a lot of upfront expenses. "DUH," you might be thinking. Implementing the necessary changes to become a company driven by its culture requires seeing the value of investing the time, effort, and money to enjoy long-term success.

Some of these things should be obvious and already in place. The legal aspects of running a construction business should be a given: permits, licenses, and certifications, just to name a few. While it is sometimes possible to cut some corners, it sets a horrible example for your employees creating an environment of "If he cuts corners, why shouldn't we?"

Less obvious, but certainly worth consideration for your success are consultants, seminars, training, and organization memberships to help the skills of both you and your employees and keep your company moving in the right direction. These can provide education, guidance, creditability and support.

Then there is the big one: what you can do for your employees. Although it is often said that money is not always the prime motivator for people, do not underestimate how far compensating someone for their contribution goes—and word travels. Benefits that don't necessarily show up in paychecks (insurance, flexible schedules, generous vacation policies) can also be strong motivators showing that you value their contribution to the bottom-line instead of seeing them as a cost. Proper compensation and benefits is a potent combination for motivation and loyalty. From the market's perspective, it will raise your credibility, give you more control over the quality of results and give you a point of differentiation.

These kinds of changes will cost money, time and effort. They may even force you to reevaluate your business goals. Incorporating these kind of changes will make it difficult, if not impossible, to engage in a "lowest price" race to the bottom with competitors. However, do you really believe you can create a sustainable company when your main selling point is how low you can keep your costs?

In the end, creating, maintaining, or changing a culture is evolutionary, not revolutionary. It is an ongoing journey that fosters growth and change to ensure your company is agile enough to grow and change with the market. The only thing in business that does not change is that everything always changes. So it is with your company culture. Not only must your culture be constantly tended to, but you have to also adapt to changes in the market. By doing so, you are helping your business survive those same changes.

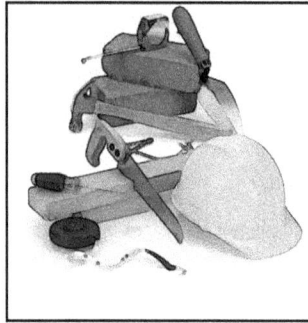

Hiring & Firing

Of all of the lessons learned by senior and mid-management, hiring and firing were the hardest. Most started off using the same hiring approach that they had heard of from someone else or learned in other jobs or industries, and because they did not know how to fire they simply didn't. Over time, they realized these approaches to something so critical did not work, in fact, for some it was driving their business into the ground.

Hiring and firing employees is probably the quickest way to make a cultural change as it almost always affects everyone else. Hiring a new employee makes your other employees curious: Who is this person? Will I like them? Will they make my job easier or harder? Firing an employee makes the others more alert: Why did they fire him? Am I next? Do I need to worry about my job? How will this change my job? Having employees in either state of mind creates an opportunity to implement a new change.

HIRING

There are plenty of books and companies out there that will tell you theirs is the one successful way to hire the right employees, and they are right. Their process or tools have worked for someone and may even work for you. But determining what will work for your company only comes from trial, honesty and error. You have to try, be honest about the results, and learn from what went wrong.

Five elements of hiring appeared consistently in the companies' interview process,

1. *Identifying when to hire,*

2. *Obtaining a new employee through referral or advertising,*

3. *Using prescreening techniques,*

4. *Doing group or solo interviews,* and

5. *Choosing to hire for culture or skill.*

When should I hire? Conventional wisdom says to hire when you have had at least six months of consistent overtime work. In other industries this may be valid, but in construction it will not work. With limited hours, seasons and more possible interruptions than most other industries, using that general rule of thumb will not get you very far. Instead, you need to look at other possible indicators and take other approaches. The best indicator is your schedule, both current and past years. It reveals what is coming up and the resources you will need. Looking back at past years, allows you to see patterns in your work flow. Knowing this information along with the resources you already have tells you everything you need to know, from there it is a judgment call.

Hiring a new employee is a very time intensive and expensive process so many companies like to put it off to the last possible moment. I recommend you do the opposite. In fact, if you want to make hiring easier and take up less time, you will need to practice the process—practice makes perfect. When someone calls or asks to fill out an application, be honest with them and tell them you are not hiring right now, but ask them if they would be willing to schedule an informational interview. Make sure you have seen the person's application or resume and like what you see; otherwise, a lot of time could be waste. Informational interviews are an excellent way to build up a pipeline of talent that can be gleaned from at a later time. You will get to practice your process, know the talent available, and prequalify the candidates, all before you need any of them. So when the decision is made to hire, there is a good chance that you will already have in mind at least one person you would like to either interview again or immediately offer the position to.

Also, consider hiring employees as contract-to-hire or part time. This will allow you to get the help you need during the busy times, learn if the new prospect is really a good fit before having to make a commitment and give you more time to see if you are really in a position to hire another employee.

I am ready to hire. Should I hire a referral from an employee or someone who came to us through our advertisement? Both approaches have their upsides and downsides. Most of the companies interviewed would communicate a new position to their employees first to see if they knew of anyone interested, then they would release it to organizations they belong to and then finally the public.

When dealing with a referral, companies often assume that the prospect will have a similar work ethic as the employee who referred them. This may or may not be the case. Yes the prospect could be a friend or family member of the employee, but it could also be just someone they met at the store. Even if the prospect is a friend or family member, it does not mean their work ethic or personality will be what you desire—think about that person in your family that you just aren't so sure about.

The other thing to consider with friend and family referrals is that you are bringing in to your company a personal aspect of your employees. There may be good, but the bad and the baggage are just around the corner. If talent diversity is a company priority, limiting the number of employee referrals should also be considered.

Bringing in 'new blood' can be very scary for a company. With no idea of a prospect's real past, secrets or true potential, it is often viewed as too big of a risk to take unless absolutely necessary. However, being in business sometimes means you need to take risks and see where those risks take you.

Over half the companies that participated started off hiring only friends and family. About half of those companies discovered that this approach was not a good one for them. It was when they hired outside of what they knew that the company was able to grow.

While some companies did have problems with it, many saw more positives than negatives. Referrals tend to produce better prospects when a bonus is connected to the hire and their retention; this typically motivates people to make better quality referrals. Some other benefits are:

> *1. Referrers are more familiar with the company, people, and culture. Therefore they are in a better position to know what types of employees can be a good fit and successful;*
> *2. Many people are hesitant to refer people who they question would be a good fit; increasing the quality of referrals. Typically, if someone isn't sure of the person they are referring, they will qualify the referral ahead of time;*
> *3. In many instances, employee referral employees have a longer tenure than hires attracted from other sources.*

Some companies thrive by hiring only by referral while other companies have policies against it. Again, it is not that one approach is better than another; it is about identifying what works for your company's success.

Should I use pre-employment screening techniques? This is a matter of preference; and should be entered in to with some thought as there are a number of laws governing how and when certain tools or techniques should be used. They can provide you with insightful information about a candidate which can save you time, money, and potential headaches. Pre-screening techniques can include things like pre-employment testing, job-related skills test, background check, drug test, driver's license abstract, even credit report, personality assessments, phone interviews, or social media searches.

There can also be tricks or hidden elements you include throughout the process to see how thorough your prospects are. A few of the companies mentioned providing prospects with very detailed instructions of what to do, when to do it, and how it should be done. The prospect's ability to accurately follow directions was the determining factor of if they moved forward or not. Using hidden elements can quickly weed out prospects but is not always appropriate.

If you decide to implement the use of pre-screening techniques, you should do so based on the relevance to the job ensuring you are protected from legal issues such as adverse impact and it can help you identify those who are most likely to perform well in the job. Your company's ethics and cultural elements should be used to make sure that new people will fit well and be motivated by the work environment. For example, a background check and drug test should be standard across all employees, while a driver's license abstract is only necessary for employees who will be driving company vehicles. A credit report is typically only necessary for those involved with handling or managing the company's finances.

Phone interviews and pre-screening techniques are a great way to establish standards and minimal requirements. When interviewed by the correct person, a phone interview can be a great way to clarify candidates' views on specific topics of interest—assuming the phone interview lasts long enough.

Should we do group or individual interviews? Do both. Some of the participating companies found value in having the group interview upfront; others found it more valuable to have it later in the process. A few others chose not to have a group interview at all.

One issue with group interviews is they can be extremely intimidating for a prospect, inhibiting them from showing you who they really are and the potential they can bring to your company. On the flip side, a group interview enables you to see the group dynamics and how the candidate interacts with the group. This is especially of use if the candidate will have a lot of group interaction as an employee, and allows each interviewer to hear the same thing, thereby thoroughly evaluating what the candidate said and did based on consistent input.

An individual interview (or one to one) allows the interviewer the opportunity to get to know the prospect on an individual basis. This approach can be more personal, is more subjective and generally, more information can be covered. However, the interviewer could miss key information or cues that could be caught by another in a group interview.

When you are conducting an interview whether it is a group or one to one, make sure you have a goal in mind. You goal needs to be specific and the approach and questions should drive you towards that goal. Many companies base their interview questions their core competencies in order to determine if someone could be a good fit. Each interviewer should be assigned one or two competencies to interview for, thereby giving each person an opportunity to go deep instead of broad in their interview. Use the same structure and set of questions to evaluate each candidate you interview so you have a basis of comparison.

Should I hire for culture or skill? My recommendation is balance. The companies were split between hiring for cultural fit and hiring for skill. The companies that hire for culture hire mainly based on chemistry; their biggest concern is how the person will fit in. They feel that a person can learn any skill, but if the person's personality is not a fit, they will not work out. The companies that hire for skill felt that it was too much time and effort to train the employees in the skills required for the job; they preferred to hire experienced employees, and work on personality and fit as things progressed.

Hiring for a cultural fit will help the new employee get adjusted quicker and increase the likelihood of them staying around. The disadvantage is their personality may be a fit, but you may not have a job available that fits their skills or interests.

Hiring for skill ensures that an employee comes ready and able to do the job but with no guarantee they are a good fit for the culture. The other issue is they may already come with skills, but are they the right skills needed to do the required work? The lesson often learned with this approach was that the employees hired based on skill had different techniques and quality standards which ended up costing the company in the end.

FIRING

As critical as hiring is to your company and its culture, firing can be just as critical. No one enjoys firing employees, but there are times, when terminating someone's employment is necessary. This is a tough truth that every business leader will have to face at some point.

While I did not originally focus on the firing of employees, it is a topic that came up frequently for one of two reasons; the devastation caused by delaying the firing of an employee and how firing of an employee triggered a shift in the culture of the company.

A bad new hire can negatively impact your culture and the effects can spread like wildfire. However, an even bigger issue is the long-term employee who's negative attitude or bad work habits is perceived as "oh that's just *Jim*." *Jim* may have more impact than you realize, especially with new hires.

Most of the companies have an orientation process to help the new employees get up to speed with the way things are done at the company. It also provides an opportunity for the company to see if the new person really is a good fit. Part of this process is normally a 30 to 90 day trial which allows the company to see how the new employee works, work with them on potential challenge areas, receive feedback from the employee and make a final decision at the end of the trial. A good orientation helps to eliminate "buyer's remorse" on the part of the new employee. Also, it's been reported that most employees who leave a company within in the first year leave in the first 30 days—primarily due to a poor on-boarding process. Taking this approach provides companies with the opportunity to refine their hiring process, and an efficient way to identify hires that are not a good fit.

Hiring the wrong employee and then shortly after having to fire them can be a costly error, but it is nowhere near as costly as letting them stay. When the wrong employee stays, they end up infecting every aspect of your business—other employees, clients, processes, improvements, and attempted changes. The longer they stay the more influence they have. The more influence they have, the less you have and the harder it is for you to implement the necessary changes for your company's future success. This is particularly insidious when the person is a long time employee. Even when other employees say it is OK ("that's just *Jim*"), the cumulative effect is corrosive. *Jim* can undermine or block changes you are trying to make. New hires who don't have years of experience with *Jim* don't understand why his behavior is tolerated and wonder why they need to follow the rules. If a long time employee cannot adapt to a new culture, you need to ask yourself if the cost of keeping them on is worth it.

Unfortunately, firing goes right along with hiring to build a culture that will allow your company to thrive. Accepting this truth may not make it any easier when you need to fire someone, but it is a requirement to moving forward. However, you must know and understand the legalities of firing as well. Make sure you consult with your employment or labor law attorney to verify you are adhering to the laws and remember that proper documentation is always necessary.

SUBCONTRACTORS

I doubt there is a construction company out there that has not had problems with a subcontractor at some point. Every company I spoke with had at least one horror story to share. With that said, it is impossible to say that you will never have to work with one again. Hiring employees is a great way to minimize the chances, but specialty and overflow work do happen. It is best to be prepared ahead of time for these situations to make them as smooth as possible.

Working with subcontractors does not have to be a recurring horror. The companies that find a way to make it work usually approach hiring a subcontractor like they would an employee. They look for similar qualities and requirements upfront and do not settle for one they know will not work out. They also, clearly spell out requirements in an agreement with escape clauses or penalties if standards are not met and are willing to pay for the ones that do it right.

This is not a one-way street. While the companies have strict rules for the subs, (they must have the proper insurance, wear a shirt at all times, no swearing, and so on) they pay them accordingly. This builds a mutual respect between the company and subcontractor. It also teaches the sub to raise their standards and run a better company themselves.

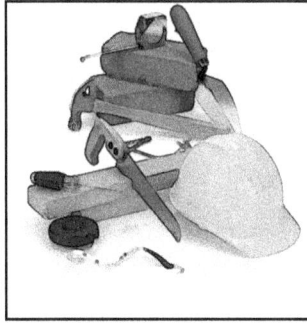

The Tribe

There are many ways to refer to the people who make up your company; employees, family, friends, team, people who work for you. Each of those terms may sound good initially, but they carry many interpretations, and may be misunderstood by some. Let's use a simpler term, one without a lot of excess baggage in the business world: "tribe."

How each of the members of your tribe perceives the relationship with other members is a strong indication of how well things are truly operating within your business. This spills out as a reflection of your culture and the face of your brand to your prospects and customers.

People naturally desire to connect with others who have a shared passion. This connection is the strength of a company's culture and the means by which it comes alive. It is also one of the first ways a client's perception of your brand is formed. Your clients will experience your brand

and your company based on how your tribe experiences working for you. "Every employee either adds to or dilutes our brand," Iris Harrell of Harrell Remodeling explains.

Without the members of your tribe, you are unable to provide the products and services that you offer to your clients. There are many factors that will influence your clients' experience with your company. Some you have no control over (e.g., weather delays, materials arriving late from a supplier). However, there is one major influence on your clients' experience that you do have some control over: your tribe's interaction with them. To make that a positive (and hopefully profitable) experience, you must invest in something you have control over—your tribe and their experience.

When you provide your tribe with the tools and knowledge they need to do their job, the only remaining obstacle is leadership. These are common lessons that the owners had to learn: trust, delegation, and accountability. Do you and the other leaders in your tribe trust that the work can be done to your standards without doing it yourself or micromanaging? "Learning to hold people accountable is unpleasant at best, but it's a task that is necessary," Harrell continues.

A common challenge that this industry has to deal with is a trilogy scenario, where there are three sides to a situation and each points the finger at another refusing to take any of the blame themselves. While disagreements and fights within the company normally involve three areas of the company, there are four main cliques that need to be united: senior management, office staff, sales and field staff. Each clique perceives the work, company and clients from their own perspective and may be challenged when it comes to understanding another's.

Senior management is comprised of the visionaries; seeing the direction the company as a whole must take, as well as the individual areas of the company. They understand the numbers, and are the unifying force of the company. The office staff is the glue that keeps all of the other pieces together and the business running smoothly in day-to-day affairs. They follow-up on the past, handle the present, and prepare for the future. They make sure everyone is informed and everything comes together. The sales team is the first face of your company that your clients have contact with. They interact with clients and prospects daily. They know who your market is, what it is they want, and how to get them to sign. Finally, the field staff brings everything together, combining the plans and materials to create the final product and being the primary face of your company. While these jobs look discrete and in some ways divorced from each other, the decisions made in each area directly affect someone else's job.

The strength of an area can just as easily trip it up. Management's ability to see exactly where they want to be can lead them to believe that the rest of the tribe is not doing enough. Especially when things do not go as well or as quickly as management would like. The office staff's ability to be the glue often prevents them from being able to see the forest from the trees. Their focus on the individual parts of the process can blind them to an overall view of how the different parts work together and come together in the end. Sales is so concerned with making the sale that they forget what is promised has to be delivered by others, and can seriously affect the perception of the company. They can perceive the rest of the company as blocking their sales by not being able, or perhaps willing, to do everything they promised the client. Because field staff is not in the office as often as other tribe members, they are normally the last to hear about news and changes. This leaves them feeling left out and ignored. They can perceive that the rest of the company does not appreciate their contribution, even though they are doing the physical work the client is paying for. They are also left feeling that the other tribe members do not understand the skills needed to do their job.

The trilogy scenario is a clear indication that the company has an imbalance and other problems will soon follow, if they have not already. This may also send a signal to clients that they may have made the wrong decision. Your clients are putting trust in your company with their job, home, and money; they expect you to be able to quickly and effectively address and work through problems to their satisfaction—not try and lay blame.

TRIBAL MEETINGS
A quote almost guaranteed to come out of every interview with companies that had a strong culture was, "We have

a lot of meetings." What company doesn't? The difference is these meetings looked to accomplish something; they have a purpose. No, meetings are not the end-all, sure-fire way to solve your problems, but done right they can offer a common ground for conveying information, facilitating discussions, uniting the tribe, and brainstorming. Here are some examples in their words.

Meeting Case Study #1: Capizzi Home Improvement. "About ten years ago, we were like the traditional contracting company where you have sales staff, production managers and installers who would do nothing but point fingers at each other. We started holding a monthly meeting where we would analyze and dissect every job that was completed since the previous meeting. Using a 5-point scale, Sales would rate Production and Installation, Production would rate Sales and Installation, and Installation would rate Production and Sales. There is no hierarchy in this room; everyone is equal. The key to this meeting were the installers. They were brought in to help us manage our company better. They helped us build a better sales proposal, build a better management system and improve our pricing. With pricing we found out that we were pricing some parts of our jobs too low. The labor would take longer than sales or production thought it would take. This built better sales, production and installation systems for our company and it connected the employees so they would work together instead of looking for ways to point fingers at each other."

Meeting Case Study #2: Riggs Construction. "At

the beginning of every year we have a kick-off meeting. At this meeting, I have a brown paper bag that says 'What is Amie thinking?' Inside the bag is a piece of paper for every person with a thought about the previous year. Everyone gets to randomly pick one out of the bag for discussion. For example, one may say 'Quality.' The team has to guess what Amie thinks about how we handled quality last year and how we can improve it this year. Honestly, I do not have to do too much work, because they have gotten so good at coming up with strategies on how to improve the business. I write all of the suggestions on a flip chart and hang them on the wall so throughout the year we can touch base with our intent. As the team guesses the reasons that I selected that word in the first place I give them gifts for guessing what Amie was thinking."

Of all the different types of meetings that the companies held, the most important to the success of the company and most predominate in their minds ended up being the All Hands Meeting or Company Meeting—which is held regularly and attendance is mandatory.

"The first thing we talk about in our company meetings is customer service" says Steve Klein of The Klein Companies. The purpose of the company meetings is to update everyone about what is going on in the business. Some of the companies like The Klein Companies make customer service a big priority of the meeting. This can be done by reading testimonials from clients and giving kudos to the tribe members it mentions. Another way is to create a measurement system for satisfaction surveys (e.g. 1-5 rating) to determine how well clients are dealing with the three main contact points: sales, administration, and production. This shows the tribe how to read a client and the company as a whole can learn how to step up the experience.

LEADERSHIP

"My job is no more or less important than anyone else in the company—it's just different", Klein continues. This is a key element in building a sustainable culture: accepting that everyone's job is important and has a purpose.

Leadership is not about reinventing the wheel or even dictating how it is to be used; it is about inspiring and guiding others to find new ways of using it. Delegating can be difficult to learn, but it is highly rewarding and profitable. You will see results that you never even dreamed of when you allow your employees to take ownership of their work. Your job is to focus on results; how your tribe gets there is up to them.

Leadership and management are probably two of the hardest words to define, let alone measure. That being said, the leadership within these companies created leaders that understood the bigger picture, appreciated the details and valued everything in between.

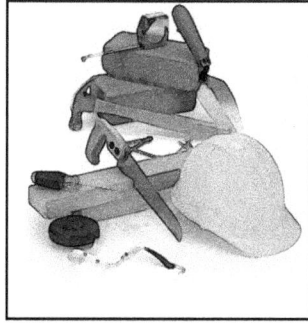

Implementing Change

The only constant is change, both internal and external so creating an environment of change will help your tribe learn to accept it. A significant cultural change can feel like an earthquake to your employees. They expect your company to be stable and consistent. They like knowing what to expect. With a cultural change there are a lot of unknowns; things may look the same, but the ground is moving, it's hard to stand when things are falling all around. What you intend to happen and what does happen can be two completely different things.

The keys to any successful change are communication and education. Be open and honest with your tribe about the change: why are things being changed, what is being changed, how things will change, who is involved in the change, and how it will affect them.

Being open and honest with your team means that you have to admit what you do not know and how you are planning to deal with the unknown. Using this approach provides you an opportunity to learn from your employees. Be open to learning from them so they will be open to learning from you. Also, remember to follow your own advice. Regardless of what you say, your employees will follow your actions.

INITIATING CHANGE

Initiating and accepting change is a choice—yours and your tribe's. Just because you decide to initiate it, does not mean that your tribe will accept it. Just because they appear to be challenging you at first does not mean the change will not work. That may seem contradictory, but successful change implementation is made up of a lot of what may appear to be contradictions.

The size and scope of the change will determine your approach. Some change is best implemented top—down while other changes are best implemented as a tribe. Here are two great examples from companies interviewed, in their words.

Initiating Change #1: No Hugging Policy. "A big element of our culture was employees hugging. That is who our employees believed they were. But as our company grew, we had to comply with US Labor Laws. In order to do that, we had to implement a no hugging policy."

"Management was approached first about the policy and the reasons for it. Then the policy was explained to the leads. After all of the management was informed of the upcoming change, private meetings were held with key employees who would most likely be directly affected and possibly even offended. The policy was then released to everyone in a company meeting. We chose to use humor as our approach to getting the policy accepted. This worked really well for us and it took about three months to get full employee buy-in."

Initiating Change #2: Tearing Up Money. "After the reality set in that I had to change everything I was doing if I wanted my business to be around in 5 years, I called our first company meeting. My guys had no clue of what to expect as we had never held a company meeting before. I thanked them for coming and explained our current circumstance to them. I went on to explain that every aspect of the company will be going through changes to ensure that it will still be around in five years (and longer). To show them I was serious, I pulled money out of my pocket and ripped it up. Their eyes got huge and they knew I meant business. I explained that these changes need to occur in order for the company to survive and that while all employees were welcome to stay, I was aware that some would leave. All of my employees were good people; they were just not all a good fit for the new culture. Four out of six employees left, all on good terms. We changed everything we do: we became an open book company, how we interviewed changed, how jobs were done, and a companywide bonus system was implemented."

PARTIES, CELEBRATIONS, AND OTHER

NON-WORK WORK EVENTS

Often leaders mistake long term results as a product of short term actions. This is where change goes wrong really fast. Having an occasional company party, fun day or day off does not mean that your company has a strong culture; it doesn't even mean you value your tribe. What it does mean is you are willing to reinforce what you already have. Is what you have worth reinforcing?

Most events are only done out of obligation; think of holiday parties. Many holiday parties are held because it is expected, not valued and are the first to go when the economy hic-ups. Employees are aware if the event is sincere or not and their actions show it.

Parties, celebrations and other non-work work events are effective when there is a purpose behind them. They are a great tool to use to launch a new change, encourage a continued action, or to reward a desired result.

Using an event to launch a change is a great way to ease the stress and uncertainty that employees may feel from the unknown and provide a start date. Your tribe will have heard about the change, heard about the planned actions that will cause the change, know when it will be implemented and have time to think about it. When using an event to launch a change, you will want to make sure you follow it up with a meeting during work hours to make sure everyone understands, has the opportunity to ask questions and give feedback.

One area you can have a lot of fun with and create sustainable results is encouraging a continuing action or process. For example, many companies have a hard time with safety meetings. Yes, they are required and necessary, but the topics are normally dull with few wanting to 'hear about it.' Also, there is often an attitude of "I have always done it this way and never got hurt, so why should I change." Using an event and finding ways to make learning about safety fun will help you reinforce these necessary behaviors. Safety is a company wide effort that has personal and financial impact on everyone in the company. Once you get the feeling started, you will probably have employees coming to you with ideas of what to do next. Take advantage of that; they are embracing this way of accepting change—don't lose the momentum!

Celebrating a success is always a reason to have an event; the challenge is finding a desired accomplishment that all can relate to and strive to achieve. The big concern here is making sure that the celebration leads into the launch of something new instead of just being an end in itself.

COMMUNICATING

Have you noticed yet that everything goes back to how things are communicated? Messages, conversations, discussions, documentation, fine print, legalese—it is all communication. Changing your culture is no different, it is about communicating and no matter how successful you think you are at it, changing a culture will test you and your tribe.

Communication is evident in every aspect of change—announcing it, conveying the intent, identifying the path, receiving feedback and working through the challenges that arise. It is also the key to success. A common challenge that the companies spoke about was the separation between management, office staff and field staff. If you do not involve all groups in actively nurturing your culture, cliques can form which tend to cause animosity or a belief that one group is better than another.

A great technique that Marrokal Design and Remodeling uses to minimize the separation is Paper Trail Meetings. In a Paper Trail Meeting, they follow the path jobs follow with their clients. Each employee talks about their involvement with the client; from the very first phone call all the way through job completion. This process highlights how everyone is important and affects the experience the client has. It also shows if a mistake occurs, where and how it will affect someone else.

Another element of communication is conveying information about the business. Every member of your tribe needs to know some aspect of what is going on in the business to do their job properly. The information needs to be the most up-to-date available if you expect the right decisions to be made. It also needs to be relevant and easy to access. A common method among the companies was to have a centrally located bulletin board where information was posted.

Speaking of making decisions, how do you decide

what is the right decision? And just because you believe a decision is the right one, will your tribe come to the same conclusion after they consider the circumstance at hand? Deciding what is right and wrong when going through a culture shift can be quite the challenge since the path is foggy at best. Define a goal upfront. A goal that is easy to say and understand. Make this the determining factor in all decision making and if a decision goes wrong, credit it as a learning experience rather than a failure.

Tom Capizzi, Jr. of Capizzi Home Improvement did a great job with this. His culture and brand revolve around the same message, "You won't get the home improvement run-a-round with us." When his tribe is faced with a decision, they go back to this phrase to determine the best course of action for them and their client.

EDUCATING

When your tribe stops learning, your company stops growing; education is vital to the success of your business.

There are as many ways to educate your tribe as there are topics. You can take the approach of reading books together, hiring a consultant who speaks to the entire tribe, attending seminars and conferences, listening to podcasts, touring and interviewing other companies, or even watching movies. It's not about how you provide the training, but who you train and when. Learning is not something that should be reserved for senior management when you are in this bind or that; it is to your benefit to share it with everyone, on an ongoing basis.

Common topics that the companies focused on were educating their tribe about running a business and understanding the financials. For each of them in time, this resulted in an entire tribe with a business owner mentality. The tribe knew and understood why and how to make decisions that were mutually beneficial to the client and the business. It was also was a great tool to unite the tribe, eliminating the perception that the owner gets all of the money.

Should your company be an open book company? That choice is up to you, but the companies that were open (to some degree) and educated their employees about what the numbers meant were stronger overall. Giving employees the 'why' information, allows them to understand the reason behind the work, enabling them to make the right decisions on their own, resulting in lower costs and greater client satisfaction. It is about allowing your tribe access to the numbers relative to their job and an understanding of what the numbers mean.

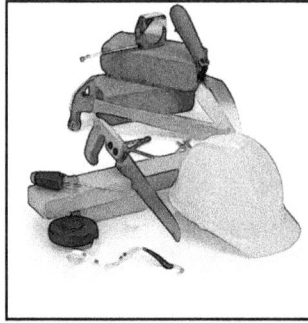

What Is Your Brand?

It is interesting to listen to companies explain their 'brand' and marketing. Some clearly know what they are doing and others just as clearly have no clue but are convinced they do. A brand is the on-going perception of value that the company (or product) holds regardless of who owns or runs the company. I do have to burst a bubble upfront, there is no clear cut path to create a successful brand. Sorry to disappoint you. The reality of marketing is that you have to find what works for your company and just because it works today does not mean it will work tomorrow. Campaigns, strategies, and forms of media that are highly successful for one company may only be an expense (time and/or money) for you.

There are foundational elements of branding and marketing that do apply to all companies. Understanding and knowing how these elements affect your brand which in turn affects your culture is vital. Before I get into these foundational elements, I would like to share how the companies that participated in my research handled this aspect of the review.

All of the companies were asked to fill out a company profile which included their financials and detailed descriptions of who their target market and clientele were. In the interviews they were asked if their company came up in general conversation, what would be said. About twelve percent of the companies gave answers that were consistent across the profile, from all employees who were interviewed, and in the employee survey. The same specific message came across or the stories they related shared the same specific point.

Over half of the companies, wrote a very vague or general answer regarding their target market on the profile which is just a way of saying they did not know. Sometimes senior leadership or the person in charge of marketing could be specific but the other employees either guessed or told me about a marketing campaign they knew about. You may be thinking, "Well as long as whoever is doing the marketing knows that is all that matters." To a degree, that's right, but if you believe that, you risk missing out on the true value of having a strong culture. When you have a strong culture, you end up with strong and smart employees—ones that understand YOUR business. When they understand your business, they are better able to communicate what the company does, identify who is a good client and make your company look like a desirable place to work. Those key elements make marketing more successful and hiring easier.

Foundational Elements. Knowing and utilizing the foundational elements will save your company time and money when it comes to getting your message out. Keep in mind that these are foundation elements that are meant to be built upon, modified, and do mature over time.

Who are your clients? What is your target market?

"People who want custom residential work: new and remodel" is not a good answer to this. Take a good look at who your clients are and try to be as specific as possible. Where are they located? What kinds of work do they have done? Do they have kids? How old are the kids when the work is requested? When is interest first expressed? When is a decision made? Are there hobbies or organizations that are prevalent across your client base?

Identifying this information will provide you with insight into who your clients are and commonalities that they share. Ideally you should be focusing on clients that you would want to work with again and what made them so attractive to you. Being in business is about providing a client with a memorable experience worthy of sharing, but at the same time it is also about working with the clients that provide value to the company. Not all clients are good ones and it is ok to refer work to other businesses.

What message do they want to hear?

Notice the wording, "What message do your clients want to hear?" There is a big difference between what they want to hear and what you want them to hear. To identify this, you will need to ask them some questions and be prepared to hear the good, the bad and the ugly with grace. Probing questions and extreme listening are the tools to accomplish this task.

Some questions you may want to consider asking are: why did you choose to do business with us? Why did you choose not to do business with us? What was the most memorable experience? What would you say is our strength? What could we do differently that would make your experience better?

When do they want to hear it?

This is the million dollar question! No one wants to be sold to or voluntarily watches or listens to a commercial or an advertisement. This being said, you still need to find ways to get in front of your audience so they know you exist. What information can you provide to your audience that they will openly receive? Make sure you also consider how they want to receive the information. Conveying the right information using the wrong media will get you the same results as not doing anything at all.

What do you need them to know?

There is always information that a company has to share with the market. Whether it is a new product, service or employee, it could be a special you are offering or even educational information. This is the information that the market needs to know so they will choose to do business with you.

It can sometimes be easier to identify what doesn't work instead of what does. So instead of asking "What do I do?" try asking "What hasn't worked and figure out why didn't it work?" When you know what doesn't work and why it doesn't work, it is easier to build stronger campaigns with the medias that do work, for you.

Let's identify what not to do before you create what does work. Here are some phrases that you should never use in an attempt to differentiate yourself: full service, customer service, cheap, or low-cost. What does full service mean? Even if you can answer that, most likely the market cannot so do not waste your time educating them on what full service is to you when you can be educating them on other more important things. Customer service, that is a given no matter what the industry or company is. Unless you are going to Ed Debevic's or Dick's Last Resort, people expect that you will provide high quality respectful customer service. As for cheap or low-cost, your clients will only remain with you as long as you continue to be just that. When it comes time to raise your prices, you will upset more people than you will be able to attract and it will cost you more to change your approach.

Appearance: Is the design or presentation of your materials appealing to them?

Make sure that the design of your logo and materials is consistent and done in a design that your market finds appealing and attractive. If the design of your materials is not appealing to the market you are targeting you will attract a different audience, most likely not one you wanted to work with. Working with a designer will save you a lot of money in the end.

Here are a few case studies from the companies that participated.

Marketing Case Study #1: Riggs Construction. Riggs took the growing weakness of the economy and turned it into a strength for a marketing campaign they launched. The campaign was titled "Yes I Can!" At a time that everyone in the media was saying no, they chose to say "Yes" and encouraged their clients to say "Yes" as well. This campaign ended up winning the Marketing Excellence Award through the American Marketing Association.

Marketing Case Study #2: Capizzi Home Improvement. Tom Capizzi Jr. noticed the frustration that people felt when dealing with construction companies— the uncertainty, distrust, and confusion around topics like, is this a good company, will they do quality work and will they complete the job? He knew that the answer to all of those questions was "yes" for his company, but he needed to make believers out of the market. To do this, they launched the campaign, "Capizzi Home Improvement where you won't get the home improvement runaround."

This campaign became the driving force behind all of their marketing and a cornerstone of the Capizzi culture. Should a client say they feel like they are getting the runaround, sirens go off and everyone steps up to the plate to find out what went wrong and how they can fix it, NOW.

Marketing Case Study #3: Marrokal Design and Remodeling. In 2008, when southern California was hit by wild fires, Marrokal Design and Remodeling took a unique approach to helping the victims. They sent out the following letter and held true to their word. They did not put the victims on their mailing list or solicit them in any way.

Dear Neighbor,

From all of the Marrokal Design and Remodeling team, we would like to express how sorry that we are that you have lost your home and your belongings.

We have been a residential remodeling company in your community for 27 years and we have been fortunate enough to have worked with many of your neighbors. While we are not able to assist you by rebuilding homes, we would like to help you and your family as you start rebuilding your homes and your lives.

While several funds have been established to assist with the recovery effort, we would rather reach out to the families who were directly affected by this tragic event.

Please phone our office at 619-441-9300, we will send you a $50.00 gift card to Bed, Bath & Beyond. No strings attached.

Sincerely,

Gary Marrokal, President

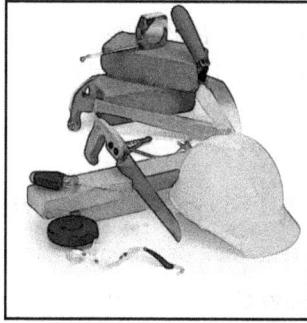

Unrealized Ideas

*I don't view a home purchase any different
than the purchase of a fish taco. It's a product!
Your client has to feel welcome and appreciated.
They need to get what you told them they are
going to get, they need to have a good experience,
leave happy, and be told 'thank you' when
they leave. Only then will they come back.*

*The problem with the home building business
is they do not view this business as a repeat
business because most people only build one
custom home. So they don't see the value in
building a relationship for repeat business.*

*If I do not provide you with the most enjoyable,
controlled experience in designing, building,
and moving into your new home, and if I
don't taking care of you afterwards, I will
never have the opportunity to do the same*

thing for all of the people you network with.
Steve Klein from The Klein Companies.

MISSED OPPORTUNITIES

Steve said it best. You can choose to view circumstances in your business (e.g. lack of repeat business) as limitations, or you can find ways to leverage these supposed limitations. Yes, most of your clients will only work with you once, but the size of the jobs that you are doing (both duration of the project and the amount they spend) mean that the experience they have is something they will carry with them for life. Every time someone compliments them on your work, they will remember the experience you provided—good or bad.

"Can't" is a word that caps your potential. Have you ever noticed when you are stuck all you seem to focus on is your limitations and things that you "can't" do for one reason or another? It is your job to be creative and find ways that you can use those same "limitations" to give your prospects reasons to do business with you.

HELP YOUR CLIENTS UNDERSTAND

Most people who have construction work done have little or no clue about what is possible, right or even legal. What they do understand is the time it will take to complete the project and the amount it is going to cost. Even when dealing with cost they do not understand why two companies can charge such vastly different prices to do the same job. You understand the factors that can make a difference and it is your job to educate your prospect on why these differences are important and worth paying for. For example, your prospect may not understand why it is important that your employees have insurance, which increases your costs; so you have to explain that insurance provides security and ensures that regardless of what happens they will get quality work and be protected in the worst of situations. Most likely they also do not understand the difference in the quality of materials being used. Going into intense detail about material quality can result in some glazed-over looks from your clients, but an overview or a few select specifics can provide your prospects with enough knowledge to show the value in choosing you.

MARKETING MISTAKES

Most construction companies use the same approach to marketing that another company uses or has used in the past. While this may work temporarily, long term it is not going to work because it fails to provide any differentiation, and marketing becomes a race to see who can reach the prospect first. Think about it this way, if a customer receives ten direct mail pieces from ten different construction companies, that all look the same, which one are they going to read or act on? Whichever one ends up on top of the pile. This is one industry that has not even come close to experimenting with the potential of marketing. Instead of asking and acting on "How are we different?" it is an industry that only asks "What has worked for you?" Remember, what works for another may only end up being an expense for you. The majority of successful campaigns come from companies introducing new techniques to the industry. That is what gives people and organizations something to talk about—something out of the norm.

Along these same lines are the photographs that the industry tends to use in their marketing materials. They tend to be planned, expected and, honestly, quite boring. Carnemark Systems + Design, Inc. took a unique approach by using a photograph of a teacup bathtub from Japan that they installed in one of their jobs. They used only this photo for all of their marketing for a few months. The tub was so unique they got flooded with calls just because of it. If the photo is nice but represents something generic that could be in anyone's house, no one will remember it. Remember, it is not the market's job to remember you; it is your job to give the market a reason to remember you.

I still cannot understand why construction companies do not see the value in job signs to advertise their work. In fact, it seems some companies go out of their way to use job signs in a negative way. Claiming that your core competency is building, remodeling or installing something permanent and having a job sign that falls apart when the wind blows is quite the contradiction. Also, wouldn't it be nice to have a client ask you to put up a job sign or even to keep it there a little longer? That would be a great campaign—profile the client in your newsletter when they ask you, then on a yearly basis honor these special clients. There are two things to keep in mind when making the signs: they need to be visually appealing to your clients and easy to read. Consult with a designer if you do not have one in-house, it will be worth it. Riggs Construction makes their own signs and does a great job of making them visually appealing. Their yard signs are a miniature white picket fence with their name and contact information on them—very memorable.

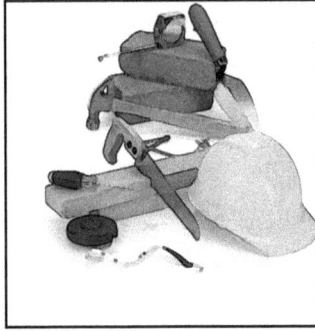

Why Does The Client Matter?

Let's address two very common and very dangerous misconceptions in business:

1. You need to take on any and every client.

2. Business is a one way street with the client receiving the benefits.

It is true that without the client there is no reason to be in business. However, a business is not obligated to do business with anyone, nor should you target everyone. In fact, a business and client relationship should be synergistic, and the clients you target and do business with should be the type that you can develop just such a relationship with.

The obvious value of your business is that it provides products and services that the client needs. Delivering that value provides the business with an opportunity to grow with each new job. Your business is only as good as its ability to grow, reinvent itself, and its ability to grow and change with the market.

In order for this synergistic relationship to occur, as leaders you need to recognize the potential, talent and value that your company provides. Do not under sell the value of your company. Choose clients that understand and appreciate the value you provide. That said, remember this is a two way street; you need to show your clients the same respect, by providing them value. Never assume your client is ignorant of their needs or what they perceive as valuable.

There are only two reasons a prospect will throw up a price objection:

1. *They truly cannot afford the product/service.*

2. *They do not see the value.*

Either reason is good enough for them to walk away from a deal. In the first case, if you push it through by convincing the client they can afford it, or by low-balling and hoping you can cut enough corners to make money, the job will quickly turn into a nightmare, and with a good chance you may not get paid. If the client does not see the value, then that job will produce the same bad results, with the client hounding you over the cost or quality of each item.

It is ok, even encouraged to refer a prospect to another company if they are not a good fit for you. This builds your rapport with the prospect and other businesses. Think of it as 'we would rather have you happy with someone else instead of being unhappy with us.' On average, companies only showcase about 25% of their work; make it a goal to be a company that showcases 100% by choosing to work with the right clients.

In the interviews, the companies that understood this value described it as a marriage. "With this check, I thee wed." They recognized that they would be with that client for weeks, or even months on a daily basis. There would be good days and bad, days when the client was cooperative and days when they just wanted it to be over. These companies created systems and tools to make the experience smoother.

As in a good marriage, communication is critical. Some of the more common communication practices implemented are walking the job, having a job book, and knowing how to answer questions. Walking the job usually includes two to three separate walk-throughs, each having a similar goal of communication and understanding. The first walk-through is with the team planning or designing the project and the team who would be building it to make sure everyone is on the same page with what work will be done and how. The next walk-through is with the client's point of contact and the lead in charge of the work and the final walk-through is with the client. This technique is usually done at the beginning of a project and at key points throughout.

In-between job walk-throughs, each company established other means of regular communication with the client. There were a number of different ways: some companies preferred guaranteeing their clients 24-hour response by phone or email, others set up a job book or a display in a neutral area (like the garage) where the client could always see where the project was, ask questions or see answers to the questions they had asked.

One thing that all of the companies agreed upon was the importance of answering a question asked by a client. There were some differences in how this was approached. Some felt it was best to have employees admit when they did not know something but promise to find out and get back to them as soon as possible. Others felt it was more important to have employees make a decision confidently. Their thought was they trusted their employees to make the right decision. Even if the wrong decision was made, they treated it as a learning experience. The employee would learn what not to do next time and why it should not be done. They understood that few, if any, mistakes are fatal or uncorrectable, and the best thing you can do in most cases is learn what does not work and why so you can move forward faster and more effectively in the future.

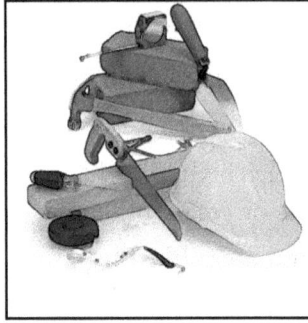

If You Read Nothing Else. . .

Here are highlights that I hope will be your take-a-ways from reading the book. I made sure to leave extra space so you can add in your own take-a-ways as well. A printable version is available online at http://www.ContractorsDoingItRight.com.

A Moment on Cultures

- A company culture is comprised of everything that happens in day to day affairs and often is not consciously thought about. It influences situations, is a pattern of the feelings, thoughts and basic assumptions that drive everything within the company and how the company approaches the market.

- A company's culture is made up of strategic elements, actions, and processes. It is a choice that needs to be made and reinforced every day.

- A common mistake often made is letting the core values and the core purpose of the company become simply words on paper or words on the wall. The culture is how these words are brought to life—how these words affect the people within your organization and how they do their job.
- Communication, rituals, and processes are how the mission, values, and visions come alive to create the culture of the company and also influence how it is maintained; creating focus and shape behavior.

Turning Points & Beyond

- A turning point is an experience which triggered a change for the company. When the business was started, it operated one way, and then something happened. This lead to changing almost everything about how the company operates, and understanding the value of building and maintaining a strong culture.
- All companies go through ups and downs. It is to be expected and prepared for.
- An external force normally influences turning points and is also needed to move beyond it.
- Being open and honest with your team means that you have to admit that you do not know something and acknowledging that you are reaching out for help.
- Losing employees is often what the company needs to move forward so you can bring in the employees that are able to take you to the next level.
- The process will take a lot of time—think one to three years with a lot of changes simultaneously.

Snowflake Syndrome

- Snowflake Syndrome is not all bad—your company is special.

- Snowflake Syndrome appears at stages when a company is adjusting to a new way or direction and there is an odd mix of vulnerability and ego.

- Just because a company has a different culture from yours does not mean that one of you is wrong, or there is nothing you can learn from each other.

- Learn from others - their strengths, their ways of doing things and resolving issues, and integrate what you learned into your own company.

- "Your team is never as bad as they look when they screw up or as good as they look when they succeed." The same is true for companies.

The Cost of Culture

- Implementing the necessary changes to become a company driven by its culture requires seeing the value of investing the time, effort, and money to enjoy long-term success.
- Proper compensation and benefits is a potent combination for motivation and loyalty.
- Creating, maintaining, or changing a culture is evolutionary, not revolutionary.
- Your culture must be constantly tended to, and also adapt to changes in the market.

Hiring & Firing

- Hiring and firing employees is probably the quickest way to make a cultural change as it almost always affects everyone else.
- To make hiring easier and take up less time, practice the process—practice makes perfect. When someone calls or asks to fill out an application, be honest with them and tell them you are not hiring right now and ask them if they are interested in scheduling an informational interview.
- Something to consider when hiring friends and family referrals is that you are bringing in to your company a personal aspect of your employees. There may be good, but the bad and the baggage are just around the corner.
- Using hidden elements will quickly weed out prospects but are not always appropriate.
- Being in business sometimes means you need to take risks and see where those risks take you.
- Some companies thrive by hiring only by referral while other companies have policies against it.
- When you are conducting an interview whether it is a group or a one to one interview, make sure you have a goal in mind.
- When the wrong employee stays, they end up infecting every aspect of your

business—other employees, clients, processes, improvements, and attempted changes.

- Having a good orientation process helps new employees get up to speed with the way things are done at the company and allows the company to see if the new person really is a good fit.

- Firing goes right along with hiring to build a culture that will allow your company to thrive.

- Hiring the wrong employee and then shortly after having to fire them can be a costly error, but it is nowhere near as costly as letting them stay.

- Approach hiring a subcontractor like you would an employee. Look for similar qualities and requirements upfront and do not settle for one you know will not work out.

- Have strict rules for the subs, (they must have the proper insurance, wear a shirt at all times, no swearing, and so on) and pay them accordingly. This builds mutual respect and teaches the sub to raise their standards and to run a better company themselves.

89 | If You Read Nothing Else . . .

The Tribe

- Your tribe is a reflection of your culture and the face of your brand.
- Your clients experience your brand and your company based on how your tribe experiences working for you.
- Do you and the other leaders in your tribe trust that the work can be done to your standards without doing it yourself or micromanaging?
- While disagreements and fights within the company normally involve three areas of the company, there are four main cliques that need to be united: senior management, office staff, sales and field staff.
- The strength of an area of the company (senior management, office staff, sales and field staff) can just as easily trip it up.
- The 'trilogy scenario' is a clear indication that the company has an imbalance and other problems will soon follow, if they have not already. This may also send a signal to clients that they may have made the wrong decision.
- Meetings are not the end all, sure-fire way to solve your problems, but done right they can offer a common ground for conveying information, discussions, uniting the tribe, and brainstorming.
- Of all the different types of meetings held, the most important to the success of

a company ended up being the All Hands Meeting or Company Meeting—which is held regularly and attendance is mandatory.

- Everyone's job is important and has a purpose.
- Leadership is not about reinventing the wheel or even dictating how it is to be used; it is about inspiring and guiding others to find new ways of using it.
- Delegating can be difficult to learn, but it is highly rewarding and profitable.

Implementing Change

- The keys to any successful change are communication and education.
- Be open and honest with your tribe about the change.
- Initiating and accepting change is a choice—yours and your tribe's.
- Often leaders mistake long term results as a product of short term actions.
- A company event only reinforces what you already have.
- A company event is a great tool to use to launch a new change, encourage a continued action, or to reward a desired result.
- Make sure that a celebration leads into the launch of something new instead of just being an end in itself.
- It's all about communication and no matter how successful you think you are at it, changing a culture will put you and your tribe to the test.
- A Paper Trail Meeting follows the path of jobs. Each employee talks about their involvement with the client; from the very first phone call all the way through job completion. This process highlights how everyone is important and affects the experience the client has. It also shows if a mistake occurs, where and how it will affect someone else.

- Every member of your tribe needs to know some aspect of what is going on in the business to do their job properly.
- Deciding what is right and wrong when going through a culture shift can be quite the challenge since the path is foggy at best.
- When your tribe stops learning, your company stops growing; education is vital to the success of your business.
- Learning is not something that should be reserved for senior management when you are in this bind or that; it is to your benefit to share it with everyone, on an ongoing basis.

What is Your Brand?

- A brand is the on-going perception of value that the company (or product) holds regardless of who owns or runs the company.
- The reality of marketing is that you have to find what works for your company and just because it works today does not mean it will work tomorrow.
- When you have a strong culture, you end up with strong and smart employees—ones that understand YOUR business. When they understand your business, they are better able to communicate the value of the company, identify who is a good client and make your company look like a desirable place to work.
- Being in business is about providing a client with a memorable experience worthy of sharing, but at the same time it is also about working with the clients that provide value to the company.
- Not all clients are good ones and it is ok to refer work to other businesses.
- Always be prepared to hear the good, the bad and the ugly with grace.
- When you know what doesn't work and why it doesn't work, it is easier to build stronger campaigns with the various media that do work, for you.
- Conveying the right information using the wrong media will get you the same

results as not doing anything at all.

- Some phrases that you should never use in an attempt to differentiate yourself: full service, customer service, cheap, or low-cost.

Unrealized Ideas

- You can choose to view circumstances in your business (e.g., lack of repeat business) as limitations, or you can find ways to leverage these supposed limitations.
- "Can't" is a word that caps your potential.
- It is your job to educate your prospect on why these differences are important and worth paying for.
- Instead of asking and acting on "How are we different?" it is an industry that only asks "What has worked for you?"
- The majority of successful campaigns come from companies introducing new techniques to the industry. That is what gives people and organizations something to talk about—something out of the norm.
- If the photos you use are nice but represents something generic that could be in anyone's house, no one will remember it.
- It is not the market's job to remember you; it is your job to give the market a reason to remember you.
- Claiming that your core competency is building, remodeling or installing something permanent and having a job sign that falls apart when the wind blows is quite the contradiction.

Why Does The Client Matter?

- Without the client there is no reason to be in business.
- A business is not obligated to do business with anyone, nor should you target everyone.
- Your business is only as good as its ability to grow and reinvent itself in conjunction with growth and changes in the market.
- Never assume your client is ignorant of their needs or what constitutes value to them.
- It is ok, even encouraged to refer a prospect to another company if they are not a good fit for you. This builds your rapport with the prospect and other businesses. Think of it as 'we would rather have you happy with someone else instead of being unhappy with us.'
- The most common communication practices implemented are walking the job, having a job book, and knowing how to answer questions.
- Even if the wrong decision was made, it's ok because your tribe would learn what not to do next time and why it should not be done.

99 | If You Read Nothing Else . . .

Melanie DePaoli, or Mel, as she is known by her clients and friends, works with companies, schools, government clients and individuals. Her experience includes organizational culture, branding, operations and self-publishing.

She has in-depth knowledge of how culture, branding and operations intersect and impact a company's bottom line. She provides anecdotal and research-based information, unique to each client, which enables them to understand how subtle changes can be implemented to ensure long-term business success.

She speaks on topics about the influence of culture and brand, understanding customer experience, social media, and creating a contagious culture mindset.

- Visit **www.ContractorsDoingItRight.com** for more information about this book, to download the free chapter, and find more resources that will help your company.

- Visit **www.MelDePaoli.com** to learn more about Ms. DePaoli or to book her as a speaker at one of your events.

- Visit **www.Omicle.com** for more information on how Ms. DePaoli can help your business connect your culture and brand for sustainable success.